DON'T CALL ME SKIPPY

A proportion of royalties from the sale of this book goes
directly to The Kangaroo Sanctuary, Alice Springs

kangaroosanctuary.com

DON'T CALL ME SKIPPY

Life lessons from tough kangaroos

Dominic Knight

ALLEN&UNWIN
SYDNEY·MELBOURNE·AUCKLAND·LONDON

'When you have great outer strength,
great inner strength is easy.'

'Give 121%, because that's 110% of 110%.'

'Nothing is truly impossible until you've tried, and proven that it is.'

'I'm not sleeping,
I'm doing reps of my dreams.'

'Every day I ask myself what
I'll ask myself tomorrow.'

'Don't achieve someone else's goals.
Score own goals.'

'It is better to eat a carrot than a stick.'

'You never need to get anything off your chest
if you've got a big enough chest.'

'Bite off more than you can chew,
then chew it anyway.'

'You are all the you you need.'

'The great thing about hindsight is
that it lets you see your own behind.'

'Always listen to others.
That way, you won't miss it when they praise you.'

'It's better to give than receive—
but a gift you buy yourself lets you do both.'

'Don't let anyone get you down.
Get down all by yourself.'

'Make time for self-care
by caring mostly about yourself.'

'Right and wrong matter less
than right and strong.'

'Teamwork is a great chance to learn the weaknesses of those around you.'

'I don't think, I do. And when I do,
I don't think.'

'I'm often humbled by my own humility.'

'What's mine is mine.
And also, what's yours is mine.'

'Winning isn't important—
that's something that only counts when winners say it.'

'Is your bucket half-empty or half-full?
Crush it, then it doesn't matter.'

'The most important muscle is the heart. And I flex mine every second.'

'Don't just work hard. Be hard work.'

'Follow your vision, and if you can't,
try revision.'

'When my heart is feeling a little heavy,
I bench press it.'

'If you approach life with arms wide open,
you will be able to grab more.'

'Be ready for anything, including being unready.'

'The secret of my success is that
I keep the secret of my success a secret.'

'To be the best you can be,
you have to best yourself.'

'To overcome a challenge,
challenge that challenge.'

'Use every moment to be momentous.'

'Don't fear, feel. Unless you feel fearful.'

'Turn every setback into a setforward.'

'I don't see obstacles,
I see opportunities to say I don't see obstacles.'

'Confront your fears, and tell them
you're a lot bigger than them.'

'Don't get stoned to get high,
get high on stones.'

'I succeed at everything I do except quitting.'

'There is no "I" in "team", but there is in "immense".'

'Work out how to make your workouts work out.'

'Push yourself to push others out of your way.'

'If you're a big fish in a small pond,
you still get to be big.'

'What doesn't kill you makes you more alive.'

'Big is a state of mind.
Biggest is a state of body.'

'The best way to find yourself
is to look at yourself a lot.'

'Don't try too hard to relax.'

'Kicking bad habits can be habit-forming.'

'There's no "attractive" without "active".'

'Believe in yourself, and if you struggle,
make-believe in yourself.'

'Be the boss of being the boss.'

'Dispose of litter thoughtfully,
and also this book.'

The Kangaroo Sanctuary

Our kangaroo sanctuary, which was started in 2005,
rescues and raises orphaned baby kangaroos with the aim
of releasing them back into the wild when they are ready.
For those who can't be released, we care for them
throughout their life at our sanctuary in Alice Springs.

You can find out more and further support our work
by visiting us on an educational tour or by sponsoring
our kangaroos at kangaroosanctuary.com

Follow our work on Instagram and Facebook
@thekangaroosanctuary

Thank you for your support.

Love and kindness
Brolga and Tahnee

ROGER
2006 - 2018

Acknowledgements

This book owes a great debt to Roger, the former alpha male of
The Kangaroo Sanctuary whose strength and buff grandeur
captivated the world. His impact was as huge as Roger himself.

Like so many, the author is in awe of the dedication
and love that Brolga, Tahnee and their community display
to their kangaroo friends, day after day.

The author would also like to acknowledge the traditional
owners of Mparntwe–Alice Springs, the Arrernte people.

Thanks to Tom Gilliatt for a unique conceptual journey
and his deep knowledge of Australian children's TV,
Angela Handley for her digital kangaroo-wrangling skills, and
Mika Tabata for her wonderful Red Centre-inspired layout.

Thanks also to my friends and family for
understanding why I was spending so much time
on Instagram preparing this book.

About the author

Dominic Knight is one of the founders of
The Chaser, and as a writer on most of their projects
he was definitely responsible for all of the jokes you liked
and none of the bad ones. In recent years he's also presented
serious programs on ABC Radio and a silly one on Triple M.
His books include *The Strayan Dictionary*, *Strayapedia*,
Trumpedia and *The 2020 Dictionary*.

Allen & Unwin
Cammeraygal Country
83 Alexander Street
Crows Nest NSW 2065
Australia
Phone: (61 2) 8425 0100
Email: info@allenandunwin.com
Web: www.allenandunwin.com

Allen & Unwin acknowledges the Traditional Owners of the Country on which we
live and work. We pay our respects to all Aboriginal and Torres Strait Islander
Elders, past and present.

A catalogue record for this
book is available from the
National Library of Australia

NATIONAL
LIBRARY
OF AUSTRALIA

ISBN 978 1 76106 725 9
Set in 13 pt Adobe Caslon Pro by Mika Tabata
Printed by C&C Offset Printing Co. Ltd, China

10 9 8 7 6 5 4 3 2 1

MIX
Paper | Supporting
responsible forestry
FSC® C008047